INTIMACY

INTIMACY

The Sensual Essence of Flowers

JOYCE TENNESON

BARNES & NOBLE BOOKS
NEW YORK

plate I

Photographing these flowers has
made me see the world differently. It
was as if I had lifted a secret veil from a
subject I had loved and appreciated my
whole life. I offer these photographs with
the hope that they will open a new
visual or meditative universe
for you as well...

plate 2

plate 3

plate 4

It is at the edge of the
petal that love waits.

<small>WILLIAM CARLOS WILLIAMS</small>

plate 5

plate 6

plate 7

plate 8

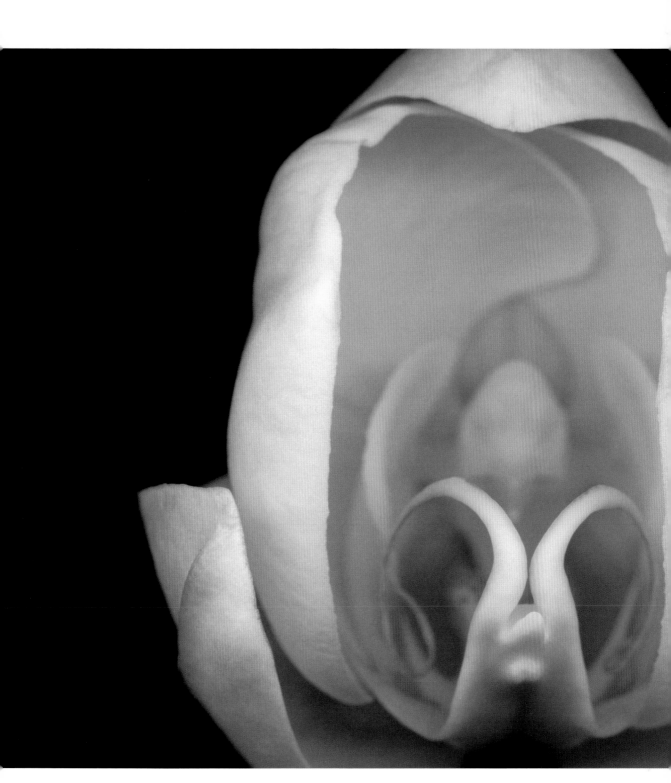

plate 9

And the day came when the risk to remain tight in a bud
was more painful than the risk it took to blossom.

ANAÏS NIN

plate 10

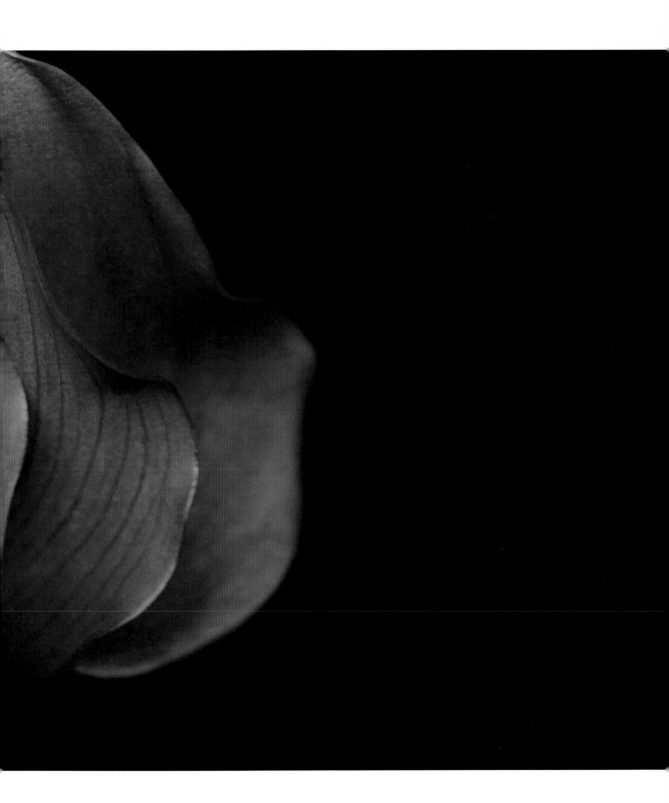

plate 11

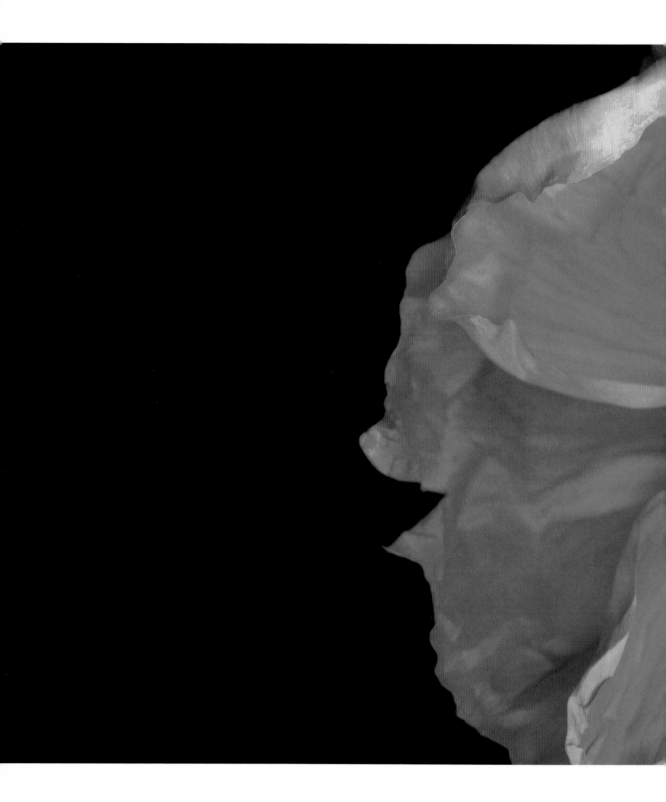

plate 12

plate 13

Earth laughs in flowers.

RALPH WALDO EMERSON

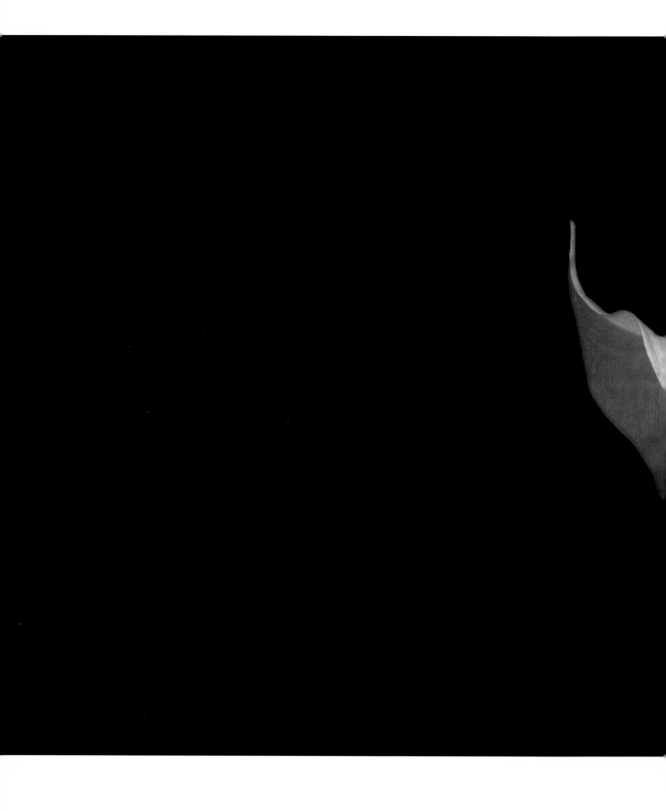

plate 14

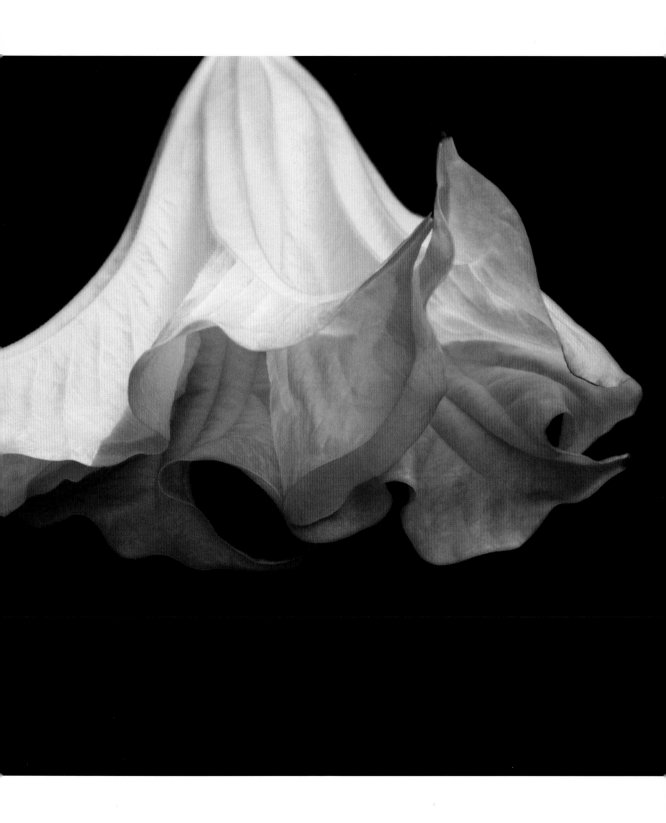

plate 15

plate 16

plate 17

The only journey is the one within.

RAINER MARIA RILKE

plate 18

plate 19

plate 20

plate 21

Achieve your own beauty, as the flowers do.

D.H. LAWRENCE

plate 22

plate 23

plate 24

plate 25

Flowers leave some of their fragrance in the hand that bestows them.

CHINESE PROVERB

plate 26

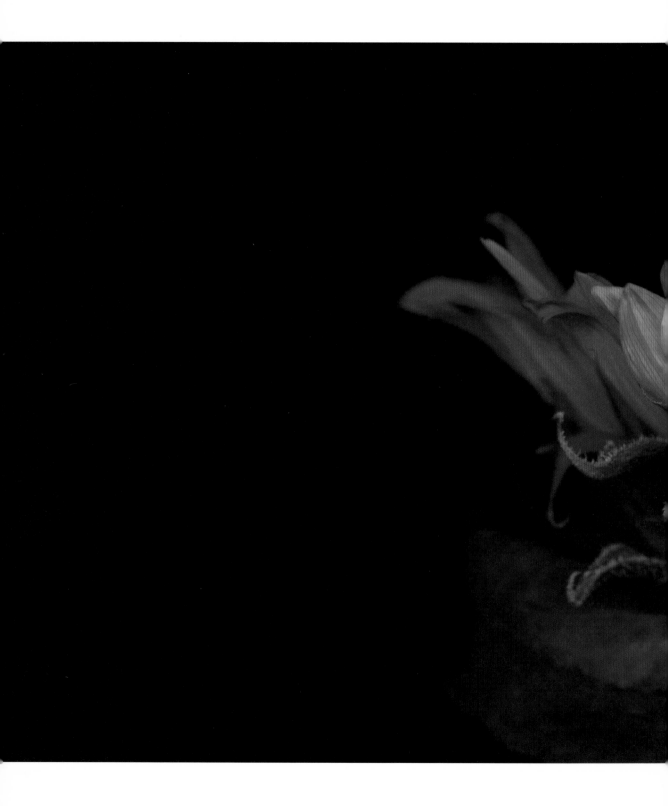

plate 27

plate 28

The temple bell stops–
but the sound keeps coming
out of the flowers.
Matsuo Basho

plate 29

plate 30

plate 31

plate 32

plate 33

Not knowing when the dawn will come
I open every door.

EMILY DICKINSON

plate 34

plate 35

plate 36

Every flower holds the whole mystery in its short cycle…

MAY SARTON

plate 37

plate 38

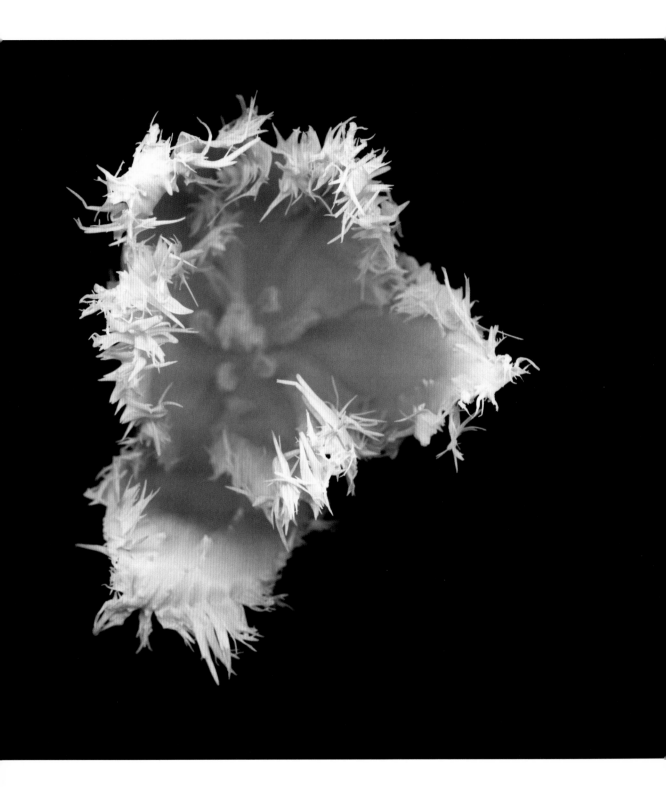

plate 39

Those who dwell...among the beauties and mysteries
of the earth are never alone or weary of life.

<div align="right">RACHEL CARSON</div>

plate 40

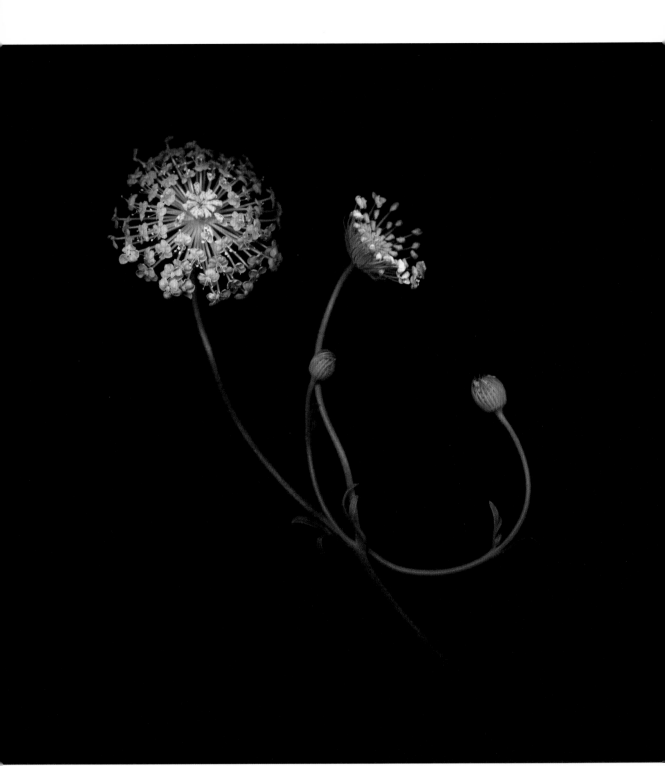

plate 41

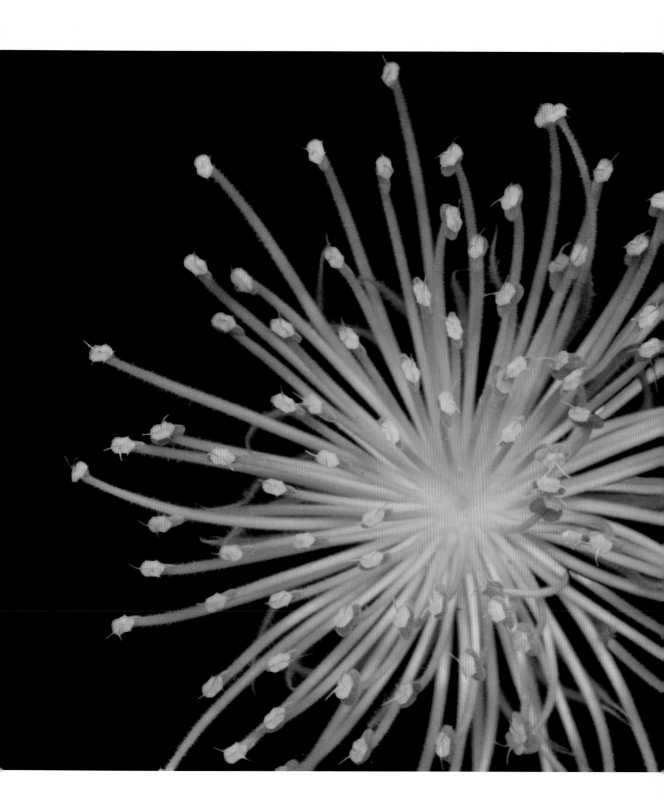

plate 42

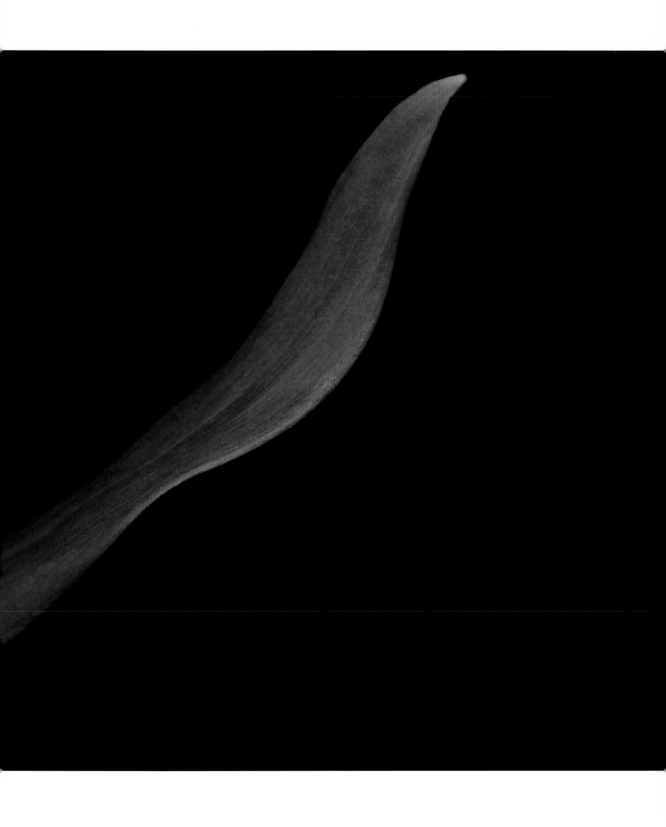

plate 43

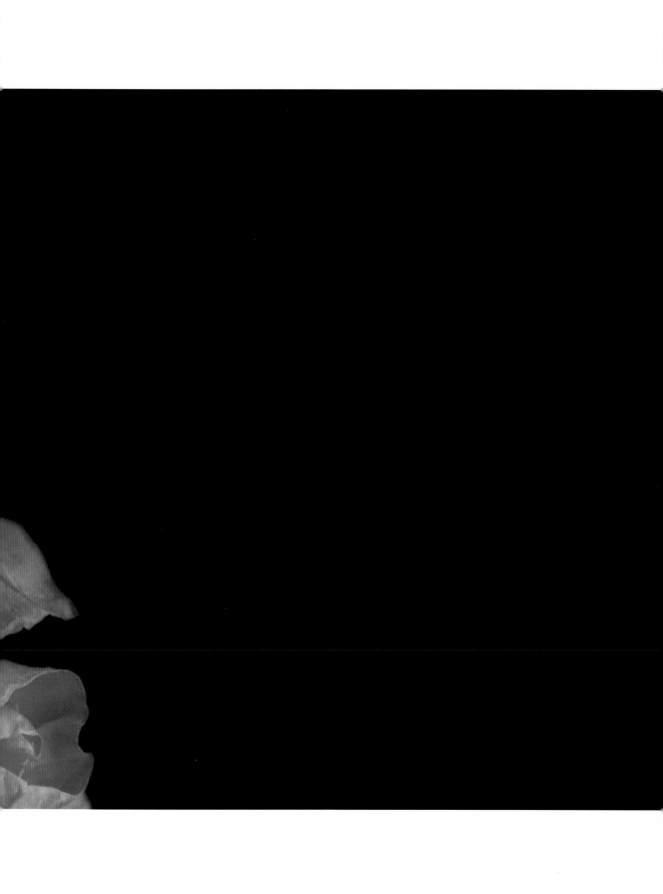

All the flowers of all the tomorrows are in the seeds of today.

<div align="right">INDIAN PROVERB</div>

plate 44

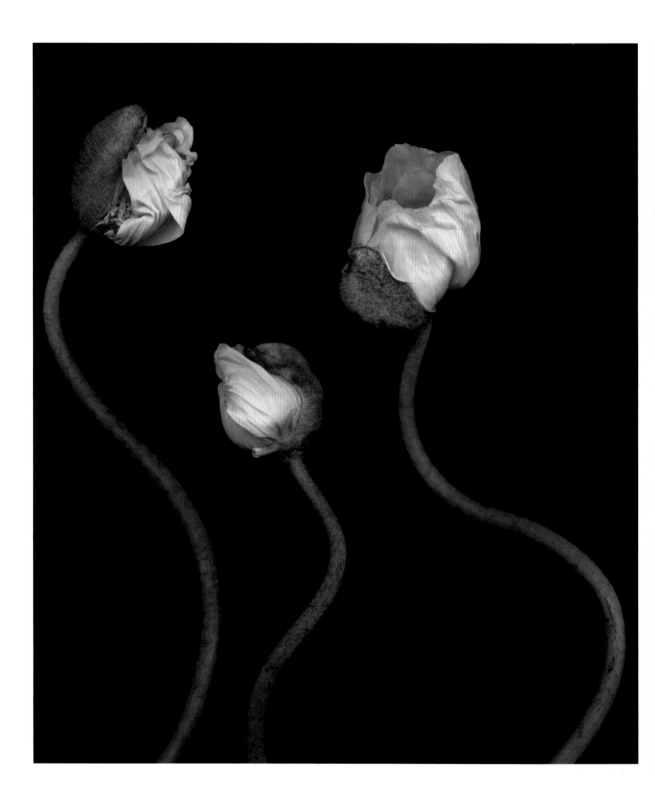

plate 45

plate 46

plate 47

plate 48

There are always flowers for those who want to see them.

HENRI MATISSE

plate 49

plate 50

plate 51

The flower is the poetry of reproduction.
It is an example of the eternal seductiveness of life.

JEAN GIRAUDOUX

plate 52

plate 53

plate 54

There are only two ways to live your life.
One is as though nothing is a miracle.
The other is as if everything is a miracle.

ALBERT EINSTEIN

plate 55

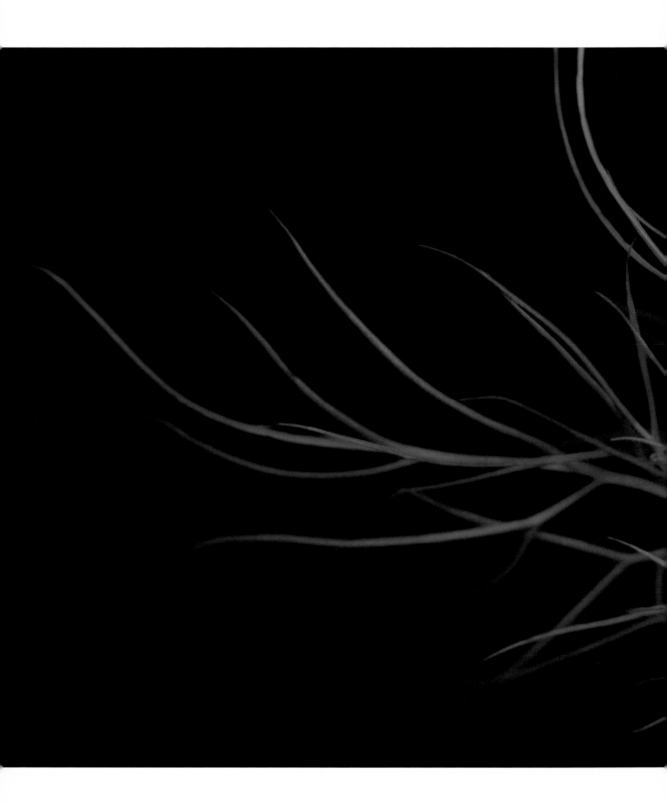

plate 56

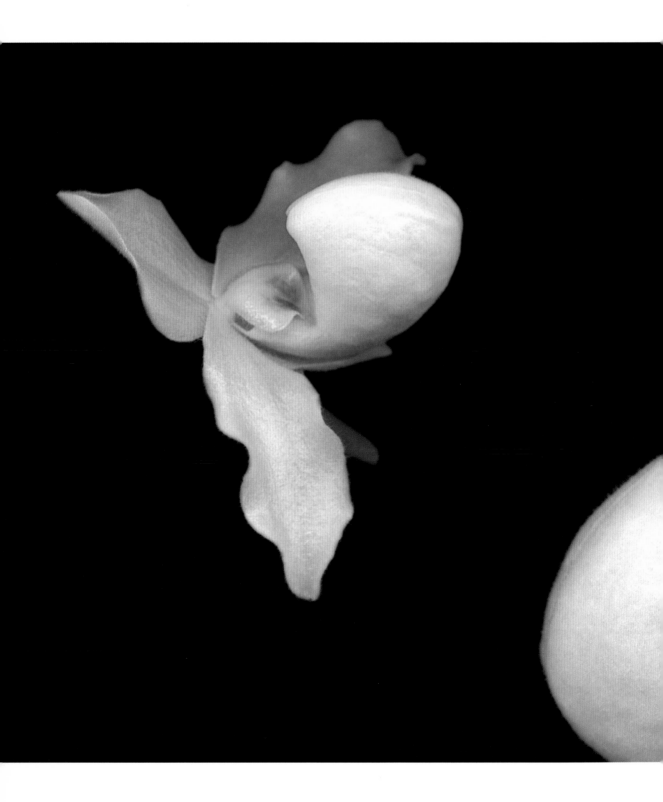

plate 57

plate 58

In the body of the world, they say, there is a soul and you are that.

<div align="right">Rumi</div>

plate 59

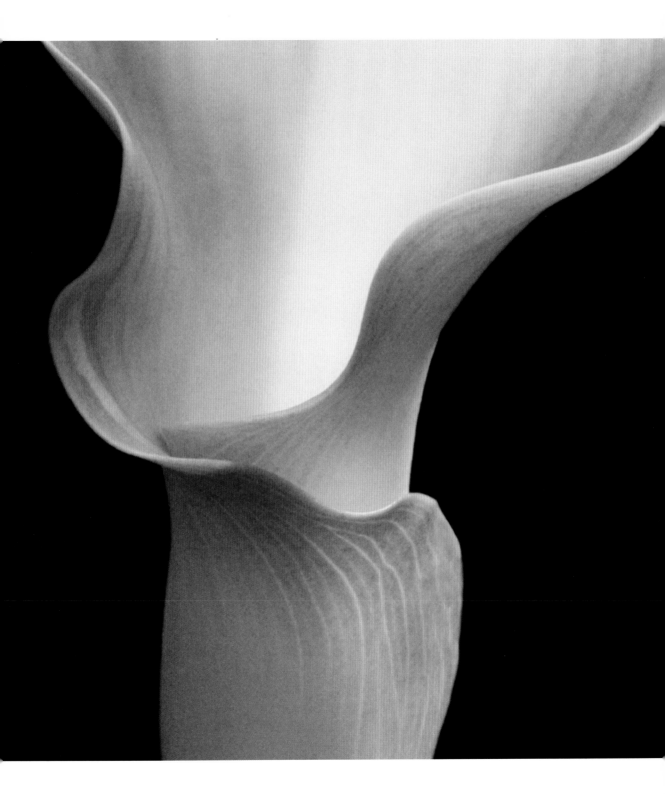

plate 60

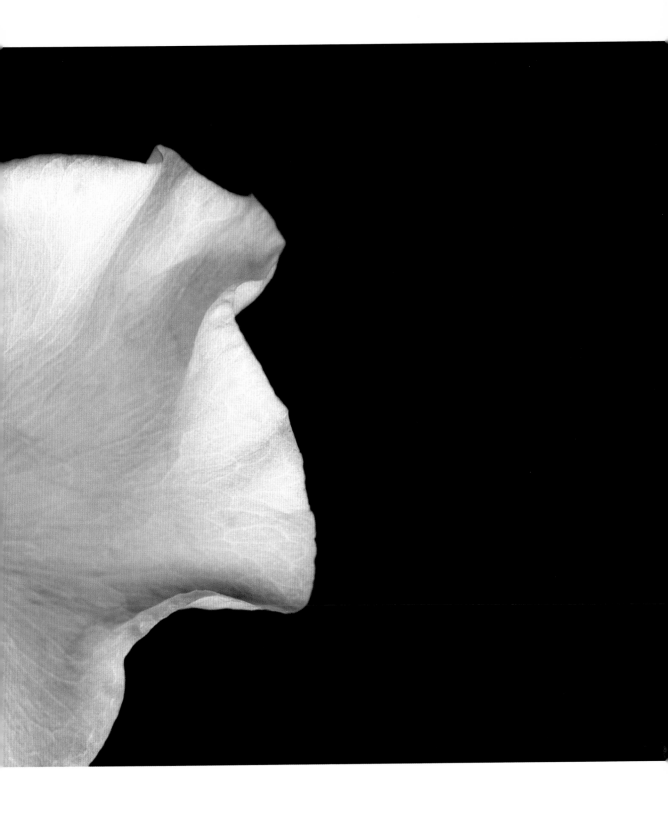

plate 61

PLATES

plate 62

The career of flowers differs from ours only in inaudibleness.
I feel more reverence as I grow for these mute creatures whose
suspense or transport may surpass my own.

<div align="right">EMILY DICKINSON</div>

This book is dedicated to the memory of Alexandra Caponigro.

A BARNES & NOBLE BOOK

ISBN 0-7607-6150-7

Printed and bound in China through Asia Pacific Offset, Inc.
10 9 8 7 6 5 4 3 2 1

Joyce Tenneson would like to acknowledge the following people for their valuable contributions.
Designer: Miwa Nishio. Design Assistants: Priscila Gonzalez, Teresa Loewenthal, Christina Richards,
Megan Senior, Diana Teeter.